STEM *trailblazer* BIOS

URBAN
BIOLOGIST
DANIELLE LEE

KARI CORNELL

Lerner Publications
Minneapolis

For Myca, the most inquisitive observer of nature I know

Lerner Publications Company
A division of Lerner Publishing Group, Inc.
241 First Avenue North
Minneapolis, MN 55401 USA

For reading levels and more information, look up this title at www.lernerbooks.com.

Content consultant: Elizabeth Capaldi, Associate Professor of Biology and Animal Behavior, Department of Biology, Bucknell University

Library of Congress Cataloging-in-Publication Data

Cornell, Kari, author.
    Urban biologist Danielle Lee / by Kari Cornell.
        pages cm. — (STEM trailblazer bios)
    Audience: Ages 7–11.
    Audience: Grades 4 to 6.
    Includes bibliographical references and index.
    ISBN 978-1-4677-9529-6 (lb : alk. paper) — ISBN 978-1-4677-9719-1 (pb : alk. paper) —
ISBN 978-1-4677-9720-7 (eb pdf)
    1. Lee, Danielle N.—Juvenile literature. 2. Biologists—Biography—Juvenile literature. 3. African American scientists—Biography—Juvenile literature. 4. African American women—Biography—Juvenile literature. I. Title. II. Series: STEM trailblazer bios.
    QH31.L44C66 2016
    570.92—dc23   2015020879

Manufactured in the United States of America
1 – BP – 12/31/15

The images in this book are used with the permission of: © Memphis CVB/flickr.com (CC BY-ND 2.0), p. 4; © Tom Woodward/flickr.com (CC BY-SA 2.0), p. 5; © mia half/flickr.com (CC BY-SA 2.0), p. 6; © halfofmoon/Shutterstock.com, p. 8; © Brian Stansberry/Wikimedia Commons (CC BY 3.0), p. 10; © AugustSnow/Alamy, p. 11; © Gary Meszaros/Visuals Unlimited, Inc., p. 12; Courtesy Danielle Lee, pp. 14, 18, 20, 24, 27; © PhotoStock-Israel/Alamy, p. 15; © Benoit Daoust/Shutterstock.com, p. 16; © iStockphoto.com/Christopher Futcher, p. 19; © Daniel Salo, p. 23; CB2/ZOB/WENN.com/Newscom, p. 26.

Front cover: © Alecia Hoyt Photography.

Main body text set in Adrianna Regular 13/22. Typeface provided by Chank.

CONTENTS

Martyrs Park in South Memphis, Tennessee, would have had many plants for Danielle to comb through on her search for four-leaf clovers.

FINDING FOUR-LEAF CLOVERS

Danielle Lee remembers her childhood summers well. She spent most of her time in the parks of South Memphis, Tennessee. To keep her busy, Danielle's mother sent her on scavenger hunts. One hunt was for a four-leaf clover. That's all

it took. Danielle spent the rest of the summer crawling around, searching for four-leaf clovers. Danielle soon knew what clues would lead her to places clover might be growing.

First, she looked across the lawn. She looked for bees buzzing near the ground. Those bees led her to patches of clover. The bees pollinated the white, sweet-smelling flowers. Then her search began in earnest. She sorted through each clover by hand. Gently, she bent the stems to count the leaves.

There are about 240 different species of clover plants. The leaves grow in clusters of three to six.

This took a long time but was worth it. Four-leaf clovers are rare. Only one in every ten thousand clovers has four leaves. Finding one took Danielle's breath away. When she became a scientist, this same excitement would surface each time she made an important discovery.

Since four-leaf clovers are rare, some people think they are lucky.

TECH TALK

"I would like to see more kids who have this natural curiosity, who come from the hood, like me, or the barrios or the trailer parks. . . . We happen to be poor. That doesn't mean there isn't promise there or genius or excitement or curiosity. I care about amplifying the voices of people who have been overlooked, particularly when it comes to science."

—*Danielle Lee*

EARLY YEARS

Danielle Lee was born in South Memphis in the early 1970s. She lived in a small, three-bedroom apartment with four generations of family. She lived with her parents, cousins, grandmother, and other family members. Space was tight. So Danielle spent a lot of time outside. She would sit for hours watching squirrels gather twigs or birds splashing in puddles. She was always able to slow down and notice things others often overlooked. Danielle also asked her parents and teachers questions. She always wanted to learn more.

SCHOOL DAYS

Danielle's family wanted to make sure she got a good education. They worked hard to send her to a good college prep school. These schools get students ready for college classes. She studied and tried to earn good grades, but she often got Cs. Danielle was bored sitting in a classroom and memorizing facts. Yet she could sit for hours watching wildlife at a park.

Danielle could watch squirrels for many hours. She loved to slow down and observe nature.

Danielle noticed something else about school. Not many of her teachers looked like her. They were mostly white and male. They also had low expectations for her. By high school, she believed that her teachers thought she wouldn't succeed. One teacher warned Danielle that as a black girl, she'd have to work twice as hard as white students. She could also expect to get half the respect for her achievements. But Danielle was ready to take on that challenge. First, she knew she had to go to college.

INSPIRING STUDENTS OF COLOR

Danielle Lee was included in a set of LEGO toys honoring scientists of color. She hopes minority students will gain more confidence from seeing diverse scientists. Lee feels that minority students are rarely encouraged to study science. "As an 'Other' in science," she notes, "I have witnessed how 'traditional' science education fails urban students."

Chapter 2

Lee earned her bachelor's degree from Tennessee Technological University in 1996.

GOING TO COLLEGE

In 1991, Lee moved to Nashville, Tennessee. There, she enrolled at Tennessee Technological University. Lee knew she wanted to study animals. She thought she might become a vet. Lee studied agriculture and animal science.

Lee then applied to vet schools. But she had a C average in biology and chemistry. None of the schools accepted her. She applied again and was rejected again. Lee wondered what to do next.

She decided to keep applying. Lee took biology classes at the University of Memphis to boost her grades. Lee also wanted to learn more about the animals she hoped to care for as a vet. In 1997, Lee enrolled full-time at the school. She wanted to earn a master's degree in **vertebrate zoology**. This is the study of animals with a backbone.

While trying to improve her grades for vet school, Lee developed a strong interest in biology. She wanted to learn more.

The University of Memphis

FINDING HER CALLING

In school, Lee studied a tiny mouselike creature called the prairie vole. She wanted to learn how male and female voles communicate. She decided to write her final paper, called a **thesis**, on prairie vole behavior.

A prairie vole is a member of the rodent family. Prairie voles dig underground burrows and runways that help them collect food and escape from predators.

While studying, Lee learned something important about herself. She loved being in the **field** and doing **research**. It reminded her of the time she spent outside as a child. She also liked working in the lab. In fact, she liked this kind of work so much she imagined doing it for the rest of her life.

Research was a great fit for Lee. She was naturally curious. Lee asked a lot of questions. But she wasn't always happy with the answers. She wanted to know more. She had more questions. As a researcher, Lee could find the answers herself. This changed the way Lee saw her classes. Her classes could help her with her research. She soon began earning As and Bs.

TECH TALK

"Becoming a scientist meant I no longer had to wait for someone to give me the answer."

—Danielle Lee

As a researcher, Lee often needs to wear protective clothing. These chain mail gloves protect her hands from sharp instruments.

BECOMING A
RESEARCHER

L ee was so focused on studying prairie voles that she forgot all about becoming a vet. But the schools she had applied to hadn't forgotten about her. One school called to ask

for a copy of her most recent grades. Lee was surprised by the call. She said she had changed her mind about becoming a vet. She wanted to be a research scientist.

Still, Lee wasn't ready to be done with school. She wanted to earn her PhD, which is short for doctor of philosophy. A doctorate is the highest degree a student can achieve. Students who earn these degrees are experts in their subject. Lee wanted to study animal behavior. In the fall of 2000, she enrolled in the University of Missouri–St. Louis.

Lee studied animal behavior at the University of Missouri–St. Louis. She wanted to understand why animals do the things they do.

NO SHY PRAIRIE VOLES

Every PhD student has to do a big research project. Lee decided that for her project, she would continue to look at prairie voles. She focused on new, **unbiased** ways to describe animal behavior. Lee didn't like using words such as *bold* or *shy*. These words are filled with feeling. Scientists don't really

Is this fox being shy by hiding in a tunnel? Lee would say that the fox was being reactive by finding shelter when it saw a potential threat.

know how animals feel, only how they act. Giving feeling to an animal's actions can skew the research results. Lee used words such as *reactive* or *proactive*.

Lee continued her work on prairie voles. But she did more than that. A few other important projects had also grabbed her attention.

TECH TALK

"Experiments are how I 'read my subject's mind.' *What are they doing? Why are they doing it? What is the outcome?* **Unlike people, I can't simply ask them to tell me what they are doing and why. (And heck, even people lie.) So, I have the amazing and challenging job to design experiments that ask mutually exclusive questions."**

—*Danielle Lee*

Chapter 4

As a kid, Lee didn't always think she could be a scientist. She wants to help kids believe in themselves and build their own connections to science.

CONNECTING KIDS
TO SCIENCE

Those other projects include outreach to inner-city kids. It's a mission close to Lee's heart. Lee had noticed that these kids didn't think they could be scientists. Lee remembered feeling that way. She wanted to change this attitude. So she began helping kids connect to science.

SCIENCE BLOGGING

Lee believes that science language turns off some kids to studying science. In science classes, kids often bump into new words. Lee says that kids don't need a whole new vocabulary to learn to love science. Instead, science can be explained in a way kids understand.

Lee wants all kids to know that science is all around them. It is all about asking questions and finding the answers.

Lee decided to discuss science in an accessible way. She did so with two **blogs** she started in 2006. One of these blogs was called *Urban Science Adventures!* In it, Lee wrote about backyard science. Lee shared basic science concepts. She explained the science of what was going on outside.

Urban Science Adventures! ©

Exploring & Discovering Nature in Urban Areas

As a kid, by sitting still and watching nature, Lee was already doing what scientists do. Lee started a blog to help kids understand that science was all around them.

Lee's second blog was called *Southern Playalistic Evolution Music*. There, she explained science using hip-hop and rap songs. The music helped kids see that science can be fun.

SCIENCE IS A VERB

For Lee, science is a verb. It's action. She believes that kids must get their hands dirty to do science. This is the only way to learn and make connections. That's what science is all about.

In 2009, Lee began working with high school kids. She taught in after-school science programs. Lee broke down difficult science into easy-to-understand pieces. She took kids outside. There, they could explore the world around them. Lee encouraged them to get their hands dirty.

TECH TALK

"I'm really good at helping people find their on-ramp to science and I enjoy that. And I think that has to do with my personal interest in working with kind of the least-likely candidate students, because I myself was a least-likely candidate student."

—*Danielle Lee*

MENTORING RESEARCH ASSISTANTS

Lee also invited a group of high school students to join her in the lab. The students worked as research assistants. Together, they asked questions and observed animals. They guessed at what the prairie voles might do. Lee was walking them through the **scientific method**. But instead of reading about it in a book, they were trying it out themselves.

The students wanted to study how prairie voles explore. So they created a maze. Then they thought of questions: Who will spend more time in the maze: males or females? Younger voles or older ones?

Before sending the voles through the maze, the students formed a **hypothesis**. Using what they already knew, they predicted what would happen. They decided on this hypothesis: The behavior of male and female voles will differ. And older voles will explore more than younger ones.

Finally, they sent the voles through the maze. They wrote down their findings. But finishing one experiment sometimes creates more questions. What if they compared young females and old females? Does the time of day matter? Were the voles healthy? When more questions come up, researchers go through the process and conduct the experiment again.

Lee was honored as a 2015 TED fellow for her work as an outreach scientist.

Chapter 5

Lee is happiest when doing her research out in the field.

URBAN SCIENTIST

After ten years of working on her PhD, Lee earned her degree. Usually it takes four to seven years. But Lee was happy to go at her own pace. It gave her time for student

outreach. It was important for her to communicate with the public about science.

In 2011 *Scientific American* asked her to join its blog network. She called the new blog *The Urban Scientist*. Lee writes about her research in the blog. She also covers backyard science topics. She writes about autumn leaves, pollination, and snake spotting. Lee also uses the blog to highlight other scientists, especially women and people of color.

TECH TALK

"I specifically blog for the underrepresented. There aren't a lot of role models. So that's why I do my outreach, to let folks see . . . a different face of science, and to see different avenues into science."

—*Danielle Lee*

LAND MINE-SNIFFING RATS

In 2012, Lee joined a research team in Oklahoma. They were studying the African giant pouched rat from Tanzania. This rat has traits that can be used to find land mines. These weapons are hidden underground. They can be deadly to anyone who walks across the land above. The rats have sniffed out mines in many war-torn areas. Lee's team breeds rats with the best traits for finding land mines. The offspring are fine-tuned for the task. Using the rats could prevent thousands of injuries and deaths.

The lab moved to New York in 2013. Lee also moved to New York. But as part of her work, she travels to Tanzania each year. She traps and observes the rats. Through her research, the team picks out the best rats for finding mines. The team hopes to produce the ultimate mine-sniffing rat.

Hero rats sniff out unexploded land mines.

WHAT'S NEXT?

Lee continues to blog whenever she can. Her dream is to extend her outreach. She wants to make a backyard biology TV show. If she succeeds, Lee will be the first African American woman to have her own science show.

By becoming a science celebrity, Lee hopes to reach a wide variety of kids who might not otherwise take an interest in science.

TIMELINE

EARLY 1970S

Danielle Lee is born in South Memphis, Tennessee.

1991

Lee enters Tennessee Technological University, where she majors in agriculture and animal science.

1997

Lee enrolls at the University of Memphis, where she eventually earns a master's degree in vertebrate zoology.

2000

Lee begins pursuing a PhD in biology with a focus on animal behavior and ecology.

2006

Lee starts writing two blogs, *Urban Science Adventures!* and *Southern Playalistic Evolution Music.*

2009

Lee works with high school kids as a National Science Foundation GK–12 graduate STEM fellow. She also mentors high school and college students.

2011

Lee becomes a blogger for *Scientific American.*

2012

Lee joins a team of researchers at Oklahoma State University to study African giant pouched rats.

2013

Lee moves to New York with the research team and travels to Morogoro, Tanzania, to conduct research in the field.

SOURCE NOTES

7 "Q&A with Danielle Lee, Biologist and Science Blogger," *Memphis Flyer*, October 24, 2013, http://www.memphisflyer.com/memphis/qanda-with -danielle-lee-biologist-and-science-blogger/Content?oid=3531667.

9 Cynthia Betubiza, "TED Scientists Get the LEGO Treatment," *TED Blog*, February 25, 2015, http://blog.ted.com/ted-scientists-get-the-lego -treatment/.

13 Melissa Pandika, "Danielle Lee: Urban Scientist, Hip-Hop Maven, Genius," *Ozy*, April 21, 2014, http://www.ozy.com/rising-stars/danielle-lee-urban-scientist- hip-hop-maven-genius/31077.

17 Danielle Lee, "We Are Not the Same (& That Is Fine): Different Approaches to Animal Behavior," *The Urban Scientist* (blog), *Scientific American*, April 20, 2015, http://blogs.scientificamerican.com/urban-scientist/2015/04/20/we -are-not-the-same-that-is-fine-different-approaches-to-animal-behavior/.

21 "Science Blogger Targets Inner City Youth," *Voice of America*, September 5, 2011, http://www.voanews.com/content/science-blogger-targets-inner-city -youth-129308033/163250.html.

25 Véronique LaCapra, "St. Louis Blogger Helps Inner City Youth Find 'On-Ramp' to Science," *St. Louis Public Radio*, August 1, 2011, http://news.stlpublicradio. org/post/st-louis-blogger-helps-inner-city-youth-find-ramp-science.

GLOSSARY

blogs
websites that contain personal reflections, comments, and often hyperlinks

experiments
series of tests scientists conduct to gather information about the subject they're studying

field
a place where scientists go to study animals in their natural habitat

hypothesis
a guess about what will happen in a certain situation based on what has happened before

mutually exclusive
not overlapping or not occurring at the same time

research
the process of gathering information about a subject. Research may involve watching the subject, having the subject complete tests, or conducting experiments on the subject.

scientific method
the process of asking questions, making a hypothesis about what will happen, and then performing experiments to prove or disprove the hypothesis

thesis
a research paper, usually written as part of a master's degree, on a certain topic showing original research

unbiased
free from feelings or opinions

vertebrate zoology
the study of animals that have a backbone

LERNER

SOURCE

Expand learning beyond the printed book. Download free, complementary educational resources for this book from our website, www.lernerresource.com.

FURTHER INFORMATION

BOOKS

Jackson, Donna M. *Extreme Scientists: Exploring Nature's Mysteries from Perilous Places*. Boston: Houghton Mifflin Harcourt, 2009. Follow different scientists as they explore hurricanes, caves, and rain forest canopies.

Latham, Donna. *Backyard Biology: Investigate Habitats outside Your Door with 25 Projects*. White River Junction, VT: Nomad, 2013. Remove your fear of science, turn your backyard into your laboratory, and engage in the scientific process.

National Geographic Society. *The Science Book: Everything You Need to Know about the World and How It Works*. New York: National Geographic, 2008. Find the answers to a range of science questions from natural phenomena to historic inventions.

WEBSITES

Biology4Kids
http://www.biology4kids.com/files/studies_scimethod.html
This website describes many science terms and ideas in easy-to-understand words.

"Black Digital Network Presents: A Conversation with Dr. Danielle N. Lee (from South Memphis to Africa)," *Vimeo*
https://vimeo.com/115862081
Watch this talk with Danielle Lee about growing up in South Memphis and how she became a research biologist.

The Urban Scientist
http://blogs.scientificamerican.com/urban-scientist
Read Danielle Lee's blog about urban ecology, evolutionary biology, and diversity in the sciences.

INDEX

ABOUT THE AUTHOR

Kari Cornell is a freelance writer and editor who lives with her husband, two sons, and dog in Minneapolis, Minnesota. One of her favorite things to do is to write about people who've found a way to do what they love. When she's not writing, she likes tinkering in the garden, cooking, and making something clever out of nothing. She is the author of *The Nitty-Gritty Gardening Book*. To learn more about her work, go to karicornell.wordpress.com.